The Construction and Flying of Kites

by Charles M. Miller

with an introduction by Roger Chambers

Self Reliance Books

Get more historic titles on animal and stock breeding, gardening and old fashioned skills by visiting us at:

Introduction

I am pleased to present yet another title in our "How To ..." series.

The work is in the Public Domain and is re-printed here in accordance with Federal Laws.

As with all reprinted books of this age that are intended to perfectly reproduce the original edition, considerable pains and effort had to be undertaken to correct fading and sometimes outright damage to existing proofs of this title. At times, this task is quite monumental, requiring an almost total "rebuilding" of some pages from digital proofs of multiple copies. Despite this, imperfections still sometimes exist in the final proof and may detract from the visual appearance of the text.

I hope you enjoy reading this book as much as I enjoyed making it available to readers again.

Roger Chambers

IMPORTANT NOTE & DISCLAIMER

IMPORTANT NOTE :

As with all reprinted books of this age that are intended to perfectly reproduce the original edition, considerable pains and effort had to be undertaken to correct fading and sometimes outright damage to existing proofs of this title.

At times, this task can be quite monumental, requiring an almost total rebuilding of some pages from digital proofs of multiple copies. Despite this, imperfections still sometimes exist in the final proof and may detract slightly from the visual appearance of the text.

Some images may suffer from reduced quality due to anomalies in the original scan.

DISCLAIMER :

Due to the age of this book, some methods or practices may have been deemed unsafe or unacceptable in the interim years. In utilizing the information herein, you do so at your own risk.

We republish antiquarian books with no judgment or revisionism, solely for their historical and cultural importance, and for educational purposes.

MANUAL TRAINING REPRINTS.

The persistent demand for certain numbers of the *Manual Training Magazine* has led to the conclusion that some of the articles in these numbers ought to be reprinted. Moreover, it is believed that from time to time in the future the *Magazine* will publish articles which owing to their special value ought to be reprinted soon after they appear in the *Magazine*.

To supply this evident need the Manual Training Reprints have been planned and will be issued at irregular intervals as the demand may warrant.

The Reprints will be arranged in two series, as follows:

Series A. Illustrated articles of special practical value for class use.

Series B. Discussions having special permanent value, or such as supply needed data to students preparing to become teachers.

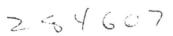

INTRODUCTION.

MANUAL training teachers generally believe that good school instruction in the manual arts stimulates in the pupils the desire to do construction work out of school, but very few teachers have attempted to direct and develop such outside work. They have often encouraged pupils to bring home projects into the school, but they have seldom differentiated between problems especially adapted to school work and those which are preëminently home problems. Yet such a differentiation is practicable and it suggests a broadening of the teacher's influence and the enrichment of the handwork of the pupils.

Sometimes the manual training teacher has been striving to stimulate pupils to spontaneous effort in school when he would have done better to have held the pupils down to organized, systematic work in the school and reserved the spontaneous work for home problems. But even the wisest teacher, in order to insure the greatest value in such home work, must give his pupils encouragement and suggestions. Sometimes he must even supply the motive to effort.

It is this point of view with reference to home work that has led Charles M. Miller of Los Angeles, California, to develop kite-making and organize the annual kite tournament which has been so remarkably successful during the past three years. Mr. Miller does not claim that kite-making is an especially good form of work for the school shop, but he does consider it an excellent form of "home occupation work," as he likes to call it. It has furnished him a means of stimulating spontaneous effort in his pupils and has opened the way to a large field of similar work.

The completeness of the success of the kite tournament is shown by the following statement made by Dr. E. C. Moore, Superintendent of Public Schools, Los Angeles:

I regard our kite day as the best school undertaking that we have. It is a splendid institution, and nothing that we do calls forth more inventiveness, more skill, and more of the spirit of clean sport. Mr. C. M. Miller, who started it here, has invented something which may be used to advantage by every school department in the land. Kite Day is a school festival which we all look forward to and which, when it comes, is enjoyed by thousands of adults as well as thousands of children.

To enable other teachers and supervisors to profit by the data Mr. Miller has used with such success, we present his article published in the *Manual Training Magazine,* Volume X, Number 3, as the first number of the Manual Training Reprints. To this article Mr. Miller has added suggestions to teachers concerning the kite tournament, and we have appended his account of the tournament of 1909 just as it appeared in the *Manual Training Magazine.*   —THE EDITOR.

August 10, 1909.

A TOURNAMENT WINNER. FIG. G.

THE CONSTRUCTION AND FLYING OF KITES.

KITE flying dates back to very ancient history. The Chinese, both children and grown people, have been flying kites for ages. In this amusement the people of China and Japan are unquestionably far ahead of us in many respects, but judging by the progress made in two years by the boys of Los Angeles, California, it may be safely predicted, that in a short time we may expect to see some wonderful aerial crafts of Yankee invention that will far excel the Oriental.

Kite making and kite flying has received a great impetus the last few years as the result of the efforts of some of the boys who have "older grown." Men of science have found some very practical uses for the frail structures of the air. These men have not only performed certain experiments by means of kites, but have developed considerable aerial craftsmanship. All these developments have been of decided advantage to the small boy, for boys keep their eyes open and are apt scholars when interesting possibilities come their way; so they are no longer limited to the English bow-kite with its long suspended tail; they have turned kite-surgeon, and amputated this appendage.

The kites of to-day are more scientific and more difficult of construction as well, but when a boy sees they are possible to construct, and that other boys have constructed them, he is tempted to try. "What an-

7

other boy has done, I can do." It is an old saying, and one not sufficiently used, "It is good to put temptation to work in the boy's way." In kite making the boy has an incentive to do some good, hard, original thinking in working out plans already prepared, and as he works on these, new suggestions, vague perhaps at first, pass before his mental vision, which he pursues, sometimes to failure, but very often to successful construction and operation.

All boys who have had some experience in kite flying probably know that

It takes the wind to make the kite go;
Just how, they don't quite know.

Without going too deeply into the physics of the various problems of kite construction, the consideration of a few of the simpler ones may not be out of place. If a boy undertakes to fly a tightly stretched, plain-surface kite, he will soon find he has about as foxy a problem as he wants to tackle. He will soon discover that he needs ballast, but the ballast needed is not mere weight. A piece of lead suspended to a string will not answer the purpose—will not give poise to a darting kite. It finds its vertical position too quickly. If we had a very steady breeze, we might work out the right attachment of bridle, and add just the right ballast here and there to make a partial success, but we must consider cross-currents, whirls and calms, and all such disturbances that a boy encounters in all kite-flying. The boys use a tissue paper tail for ballast. The tail steadies the kite, not so much by its actual weight, as by the pull due to the resistance it offers in being drawn through the air. It takes much longer for a tail of this kind to drop to its normal position and is a constant balancer during that time, being sufficient to carry the kite through a temporary disturbance, or to the adjustment of a contrary breeze. It is the same principle as the one employed by the rope walkers who poise themselves by the use of fans. So much for kites with tails.

The tailless kite must have some recompense for the loss of its tail, and this is to be found in its construction. Instead of the tight-covered surface, the cover is put on loosely, Fig. A. The cross piece of the frame is bowed, and this throws the vertical stick, called the spine, well forward. The projection of the spine to the front, forms a ridge on the front surface, like the keel of a bird, and may be likened to the keel of a canoe, also. The first canoes were hollowed out of logs and were round on the bottom. Such a one would soon leave the uninitiated on the wrong side—the under side—but later there was a keel extending

8

down deep into the water which gave greater poise. Just so with the kite. The boat is not square to the front or to the rear, so the tailless, the best of all flyers, tapers at the top and bottom. The keel is sometimes projected straight out from a flat surface, Fig. B. Kites with keels will ride a rather turbulent atmosphere, and very soon recover their equilibrium. Box kites have vertical or oblique surfaces that keep the kite in poise without the assistance of tail or special keel.

What makes the kite rise? The same thing that causes the windmill to turn; and this is true with a box kite, as well a plain one. The windmill fan turns at an angle to the breeze, and the surface of the kite

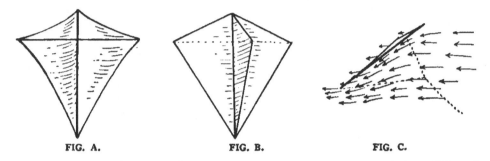

FIG. A.   FIG. B.   FIG. C.

does the same. Fig. C will help to demonstrate this principle. The air in moving against the kite, has a tendency to push the obstacle out of the way, and would carry it on away with it but for the fact that there is usually a boy attached to the other end of the anchor line. The air must then get by some way, as there is other air pushing from behind. The attachment of the bridle is such as to throw the upper part far forward and so cause most of the air to escape by the under route, as shown by the congestion of arrows, Fig. C. But the thickening of the arrows has a double meaning: it means compression, and compression means resistance; but that resistance is nearly all on the under side of the kite and is just so much more of a lifting force. The force of gravity has all the while to be overcome, but in addition to the lifting power, if the kite is not well balanced, the air will pass too much to one side or the other, and if the bridle should not be well adujsted the kite will dodge and dive and cut up antics sufficient to try the most patient. One boy tried to make a "Foxy Grandpa" kite, but he said the grandpa proved so foxy that he would stand on his head. It lacked poise somewhere.

The secret, then, if it may be called a secret, lies in the proper shaping and balancing of the kite in its construction, a proper tilting of the kite's surface to the breeze, and the use of keels or balancers sufficient to give additional poise in times of special disturbances.

9

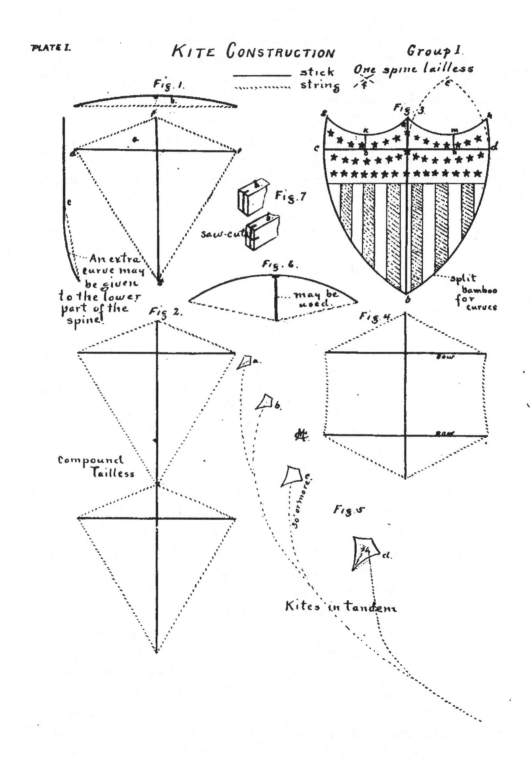

KITE CONSTRUCTION — Group I

PLATE I.

One spine tailless

Fig. 1.

Fig. 7

saw-cut

An extra curve may be given to the lower part of the spine.

Fig. 6.
may be used.

split bamboo for curves

Fig. 2.

Compound Tailless

Fig. 4.

Bow

Bow

Fig. 5

30 or more.

Kites in tandem

The framework, which is usually made of wood, should be light and tough. Some frames have been made of aluminum tubing. Sometimes a light wood of large dimensions is preferred to heavier wood of smaller size. Spruce is considered a very satisfactory wood, but yellow pine, basswood and white cedar are very good. In the large-sized kites, bamboo is excellent, but split bamboo for body construction lacks sufficient stiffness; it is very serviceable, however, in bending for forms, but not for bows in tailless kites. In California the boys use a three-foot redwood shingle, called a "shake." It is of uniform thickness and is split into sticks about $\frac{7}{16}$ or $\frac{1}{2}$ inch in width.

In the plain kite, the sticks should be lashed together with string, as nailing weakens the stick. In lashing two pieces together, they should be wound diagonally in both directions, with a few rounds between the sticks and around the other windings, to tighten the whole lashing. See Fig. D.

The covering is a very important part of the construction, not only in the material used but in the way it is put on. Probably more kites are covered with tissue paper than any other material. If a good grade of tissue paper is used, it makes a very satisfactory covering for our Southern California breezes. There is a great deal of difference in the grades of tissue paper. A much stronger paper is the Japanese or Chinese rice paper, which usually has to be pasted together, as it comes in rather small sheets in this part of the country, although it is possible to get larger sheets. With large tailless kites, a network of string is sometimes strung over the surface to be covered, to give support to the paper. For box kites and large surface plain kites, lining cambric is very serviceable. It comes in all colors, is inexpensive and durable. Some prefer silk, and some don't, because it squeezes the pocketbook too hard. A flimsy covering is not as good as one with a little stiffening. In drawing on the cloth cover, care must be taken to avoid getting the goods on the kite too much on the bias, as there will be more sagging on one side than the other. (For folding kites see the bibliography at the end of this article.)

The string is an essential part, for if the string breaks—!! For small kites of about three feet a four-ply cotton string is about as good as any. A well twisted cotton string is much to be preferred to a hemp string. The seine twine, running from 6 ply to 72, is a very serviceable kite-line. For very large kites, small rope and wire are used. The string should be about twice as strong as the kite usually pulls in order to meet emergencies. Remember your string is as only as strong as its weakest point, and a string soon loses in strength if it is allowed to get wet—more so, if it is not thoroughly dried afterward.

Fig. 7 of Plate I, shows the best way to let in the string at the end of the sticks of the framework. A saw is used to make the cuts, as the knife is liable to split the wood. Directions for stringing a tailless kite might be of value here. We will present our framework with two pieces lashed together, the bow in the middle, the spine at one-fifth the

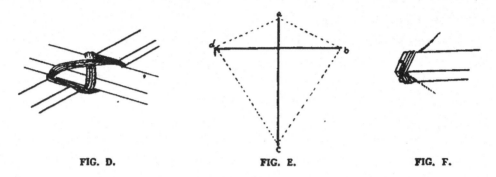

FIG. D.   FIG. E.   FIG. F.

distance from the top, and with the saw-cuts as indicatd above at the end of each stick. Start by tying string around top of spine at a, Fig. E; pass around b, c, and d. Draw it fairly tight through a and tie again. Now, b in this illustration is a little higher than d. This should not be so. We now measure and make ab exactly equal to ad. As soon as they are equal, take string and wind securely b and d. See Fig. F. Now measure and secure bc and cd, for the spacing of ab and ad will not necessarily bring bc equal to cd, as the spine may be bent.

Some kind of a classification of kites seems necessary before taking up the modes of construction. We will first separate them into two general classes, each large in itself:

A. Plain-surface kites.

B. Box kites.

A can be subdivided as follows: (1) kites with tails, (2) tailless kites, (3) figure kites. B may be divided thus: (1) square or rectangular, (2) triangular, (3) cylindrical, (4) tetrahedral. It is possible to combine not only the A and B features, but each may be used in tandem, as shown on Plate I, Fig. 5, or they may be compounded, as shown on Plate I, Fig. 2, and Plate II, at the lower corner. Constructions belonging to kitology, but not exactly kites in themselves, are the messengers, parachutes, signaling devices, wireless aerials, photographic apparatus, and many other appliances.

PLATE II.

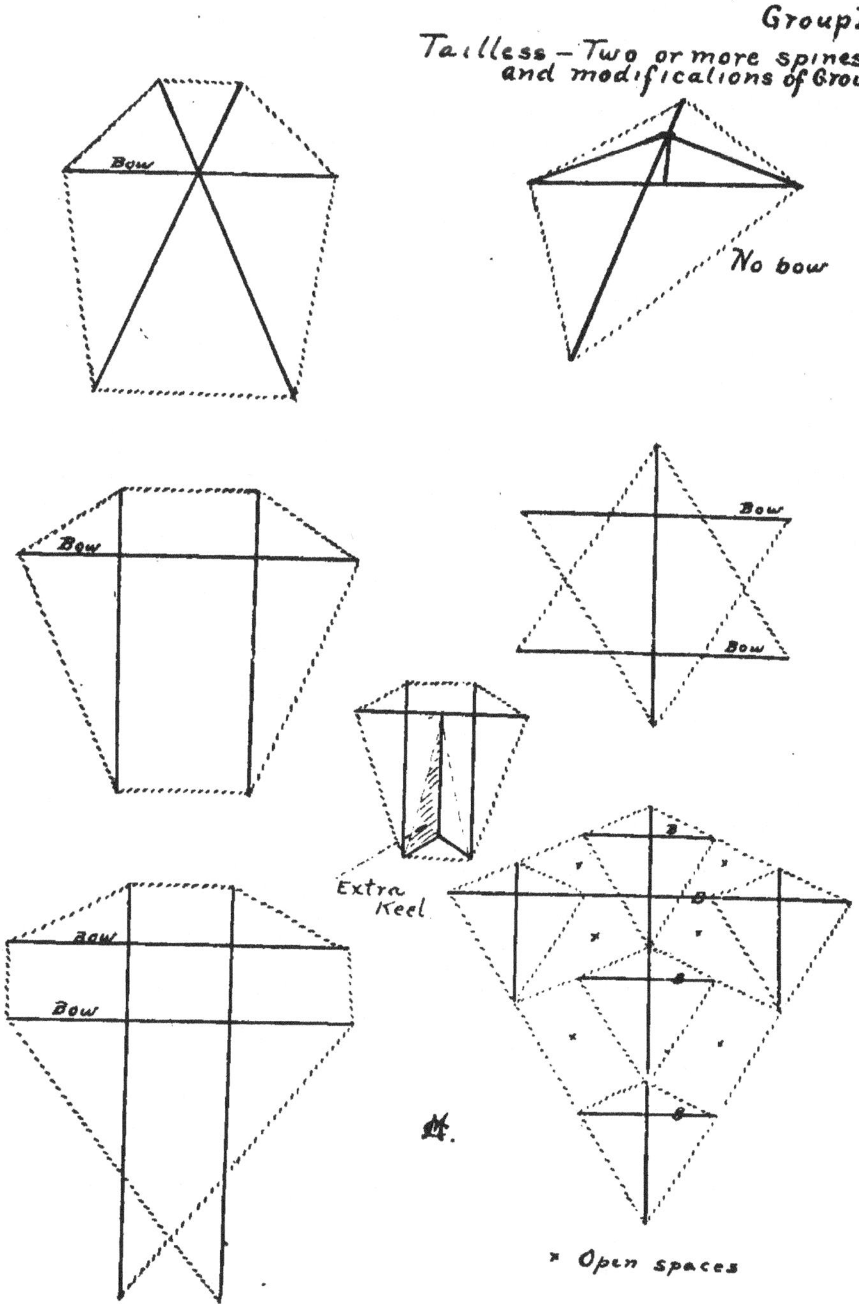

Group II

Tailless – Two or more spines, and modifications of Group I.

Bow

No bow

Bow

Bow

Bow

Bow

Bow

Extra Keel

M.

× Open spaces

PLAIN-SURFACE KITES.

1. Kites with tails have a representation in the group on Plate III. The English bow-kite was quite a familiar figure to our fathers. The construction is simple and can be easily understood from the drawing. (The horizontal stick may be omitted.) The tail is long and is made of short pieces of paper folded or rolled up, and tied about the middle with the string of the tail. A piece of cloth usually is found on the end.

The star kite, Plate III, admits of considerable variety. The cover may extend over the entire figure, making a hexagonal kite, or may cover just to the string shown by the dotted line, and both may be made, with or without the fringe. Again, each point of the star may be of a contrasting color, or there may be a star within a star.

The star and crescent is a production of one of the school boys. A crescent frame is made of split bamboo; two sticks of the star are long enough to cross the crescent, giving strength to the whole structure.

The five pointed star kite also has three sticks of equal length. They must be securely lashed together at the point of crossing. The horizontal stick can be bowed a little to good advantage. A further development of this kite would be the addition of a light circular band around the outside for the support of a fringe, which should add much to the beauty of the structure.

The kite considered the most artistic by a very competent set of judges at last year's tournament was a large six pointed star kite with fringe, and smaller stars of contrasting colored papers on the inside. The tail was made up of a graded series of duplicate kites, running down to a small one at the tip end. See photograph, Fig. G.

The Japanese rectangular kite shown at the top of Plate III is made entirely of split bamboo. The vertical and two oblique sticks should be heavier than the horizontal. The two tails are of heavy cord (twisted cloth can be used) with long tassels on the ends.

The circular kites need little explanation, but the horizontal sticks should bow a little—the upper one more than the lower. The small circles of the lower kite should extend a little beyond the large circle in order to allow good lashing. If the card board discs used on the tails are not sufficient balancers, they can be made double. See Fig. H.

Before leaving this group, we must consider the bridle. Let us show the attachment of a bridle to a hexagonal kite. See Fig. I. Take a string long enough to reach from b to c with enough slack to reach out about half th height of the kite away from the kite. Attach another

PLATE III.

Kites with tails

Front side convex

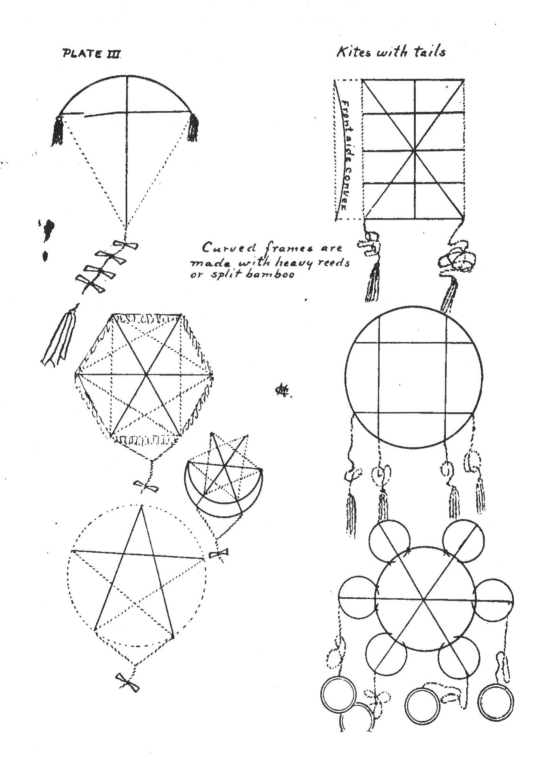

Curved frames are
made with heavy reeds
or split bamboo

of equal length to a and d. Bring the two strings together at e about one-fourth of the distance above the center, and attach the kite-string at this point. See that a e is the same length as b e.

FIG. H.

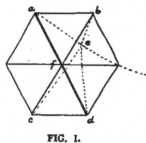

FIG. I.

The Japanese unite a great many points in their bridle, but all must be attached to the kite string—or anchor line—above the center. The five-pointed star kite would have a little different bridle. The bridle string from the top of the two sticks would meet two strings from the lower end of the same sticks, and be attached to the anchor line above the center of the kite.

Two anchor lines are sometimes used for the purpose of performing kite tactics in the air. Two separate bridles are then necessary, and instead of crossing, would extend from a to c and from b to d in the above illustration. The two strings must be played out equally until the kite is well up, then by skillful manipulation many beautiful tricks may be attempted.

Don't cast aside a kite just because it has to have a tail. The fox is said to be proud of his tail. Surely many kites are made more beautiful by the trailing of a long tail, but when two long graceful lines float out parallel to each other, you get a very pleasing effect, as they sway back and forth in the varying breezes.

2. Tailless kites are most popular with the boys nowadays. They cannot fasten the pieces together and attach bridles carelessly with hope for success, but each operation must be carefully measured and worked. The tailless is a very easy flyer and works well in tandem, or may be compounded. The bridle is sometimes attached to the two ends of the spine; sometimes the upper end is attached where the bow and spine are lashed together, but should be made long enough to reach from the top to the end of the bow, and from that to the bottom. In Fig. 1, Plate I, fdg is the length of the bridle. The anchor line is attached to the point that just reaches the end of the bow.

Fig. 2, Plate I, is a compound kite of two tailless. It has one long spine and two bows. The bridle will be attached at the crossing of the upper bow and bottom of the spine.

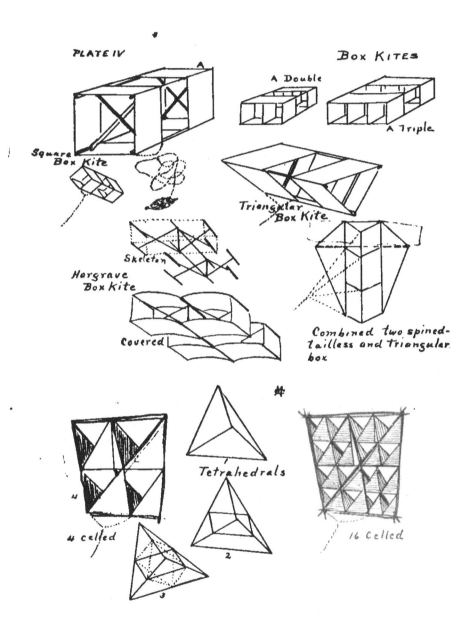

PLATE IV

BOX KITES

A Double

A Triple

Square Box Kite

Triangular Box Kite

Skeleton

Hargrave Box Kite

Covered

Combined two spined-tailless and triangular box

Tetrahedrals

4 celled

16 Celled

Fig. 3, Plate I, makes a beautiful kite and flies well. The curves g c b and h d b are made of split bamboo and are fastened before a k g and a m h are put on, but when the latter are attached, the strings at m and k draw them down into the upper curves.

Fig. 4, Plate I, with one spine and two bows, is one of the strong pulling tailless kites. The tailless kites as a rule are not strong pullers. The lower bow of this kite should not be bent quite as much as the upper. The spacing is as essential in this, as in Fig. 1. The bridle may be attached in different ways. A loop from one end of the upper bow to the lower end, with another string from its exact center to the lower end of the spine, is a very satisfactory attachment.

In flying the tandem, as shown in Fig. 5 of the same plate, the drawing says 30 feet or more for the extra line of each kite, but an hundred feet and upward is much better. First put up a kite on the main line some three hundred or more feet, then put up a No. 2 on an extra line about 100 feet or more, and tie this to the main line. Let the line out until the second is 300 feet or so away, and attach the third, then the fourth, and so on. Kites can be put up to a great height in this way, for the second, third and so on, lift the string and allow No. 1 to mount higher, which it will do as soon as it is relieved of the load of string.

Plate II is self-explanatory. The three to the left are small boys' modification, and should have a very loose covering. The middle one on the left-hand gave some trouble one day, so an extra keel was added that gave poise and made a strong puller of it. The illustration is given a little to the right.

A small boy came to me one day with a broken heart, and it was all because another boy had broken the bow of his kite. A few encouraging words soon brought back the smile, and a little manipulation brought out as good a sailing kite as there was in the neighborhood. The result is shown in the upper corner. The bow was broken in the middle, so an extra stick was lashed to the back, as shown, leaving the spine well raised.

The large compound kite has no very great advantage over other forms, but is an interesting experiment.

3. Figure Kites. Fig. 3 of Plate I is a beginning of a modification of this class. The construction of figure kites is one of the most interesting developments on the amusement side of the whole problem, but it is also the most difficult, unless tails are used; so whether tails are shown in the illustrations or not, they probably will be needed. Spe-

cific directions or comment cannot be given to each, as it would be as unlimited as nature itself; so a glance at a skeleton here and there will be as much as we can accomplish. Much of the detail must be brought out with dark paper cut to shape, or by the use of a brush. A framework that comes nearest to the center line may be best in some cases, while in others the object will be, to approach the outline. Sometimes a figure is pieced out with a piece of stiff paper to carry some small detail of the outline, but much more is done by a skillful running of string from one part of the framework to another.

The suggestions for the boy kite on Plate V was found in D. C. Beard's book. There are two books by this author that are very worthy of recommendation—"American Boy's Handy Book," and "The Outdoor Handy Book." Many interesting figures are worked out in kite forms. The two books named should be in every home where there are restless boys.

The boy kite can be modified to suit the occasion, but he is not any more obedient in the flying, at times, than some other boys are with their duties at home. The bridle should be attached to the wrists, ankles and top of the head. Each arm stick should be securely lashed to both leg sticks also to the arm sticks where they cross each other. Reed is used to form the outline of the head, hands and feet.

Some very pretty butterfly kites have been made. Here is a chance for some good observation in nature study. A little different method of pasting is necessary here, as it is impossible to get the irregular outline by turning over the edges, so a strip is pasted over the string to the back side of the cover, see Fig. I, thus securing the string to the cover, at the same time leaving the irregular edge free. This hint will be useful many times, so stow it away. The body of the butterfly can be made of a stiff piece of paper. The antennae of light wire or small reed. A light yellow butterfly with dark markings makes a showy kite. The reverse is also true.

The owl may be made of tan paper with dark brown markings. The two horizontal pieces should be bowed, and if carefully made, the kite should fly without a tail. The bridle should be attached to both ends of the spine and both ends of the upper bow.

The bat will surely need a tail, for he is too broad for the height to balance without one. Apply the bridle at a b c d.

The beetle is so near like the owl that it will not require separate attention.

PLATE V.

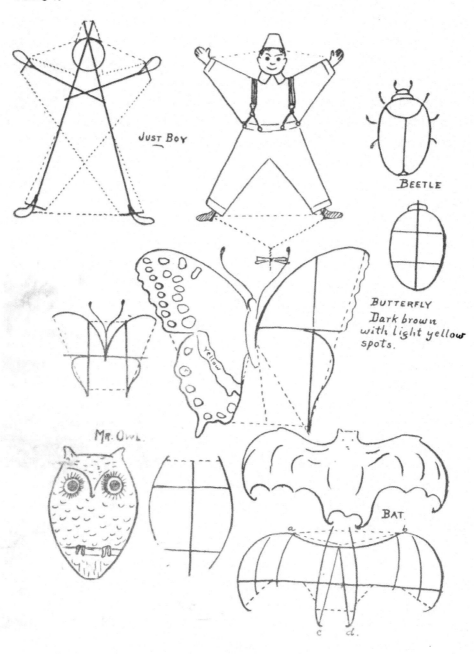

JUST BOY

BEETLE

BUTTERFLY
Dark brown
with light yellow
spots.

Yellow

MR. OWL.

BAT

PLATE VI.

SHIP KITES.

BROWNIES.

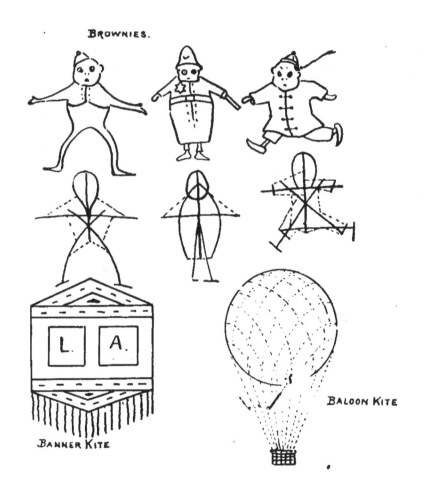

BANNER KITE

BALOON KITE

The ship kites with white sails and dark hulls, Plate VI, are very beautiful. The one to the right is about the construction given in the "Outdoor Handy Book," by Beard. I believe it will be possible to construct these carefully enough to fly them without tails. The tails should be in the shape of anchors when used.

The brownies make interesting kites, but like Foxy Grandpas, are hard to fly.

The construction of the banner kite is the same as Fig. 4, Plate I.

The construction of the balloon kite is given on Plate III. The basket and cords take the place of a tail. The balloon should be dark color. This has never been tried to my knowledge, so he who succeeds with it may send word to the writer, 512 S. Boyle St., Los Angeles, Cal.

BOX KITES.

The second general division has more than ordinary interest these days, as out of this group has been developed the most important of the air ship inventions. The latest air ships are kites of large dimensions, combining compound box and plain kites with the addition of propelling apparatus.

Reference to Plate IV should convince one that there is ample opportunity for variety in this class, too, the square or rectangular being perhaps the most familiar. The square kite is only square in cross section. It consists of a light framework of four long sticks, one in each corner, running lengthwise, and four short ones used as braces. Two bands of paper or cloth surround the kite, one at each end, with an open space between them. It is necessary to have these open space as air vents. The band and space enclosed is called a cell. The braces are fitted in about half the depth of the cell. The brace should be cut to fit the corner piece, as shown in Fig. K. The winding is to prevent splitting when the kite is suddenly wrenched by a whirl of wind. A good size for the long sticks is $\frac{3}{16}$ x $\frac{1}{2}$ x 34 inches set diagonally in the corner as shown in Fig. K. The braces should be just long enough between

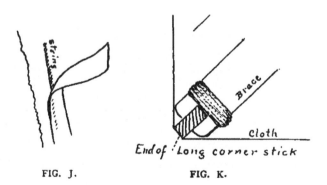

FIG. J.   FIG. K.

PLATE VII.

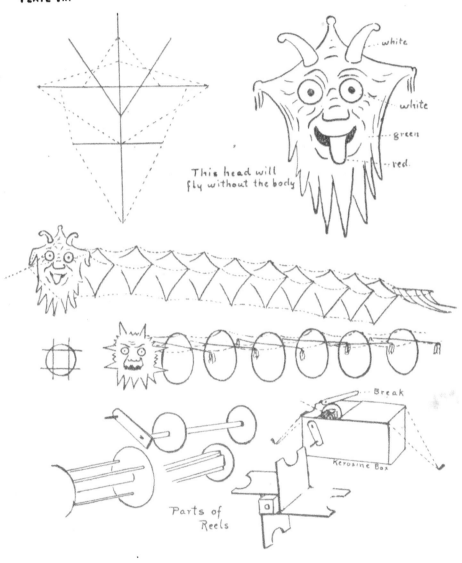

white

white

green

red.

This head will
fly without the body

Break

Kerosine Box

Parts of
Reels

notches to necessitate their being sprung into place. Shallow notches should be cut in the long sticks to receive the braces. The covering we will suppose to be of cloth, the kite to be 16 inches square. It will require a strip 64 inches long plus 1 inch for seam. The two edges should have a ½ inch hem, and the cell should be 9 inches wide; so to allow for the two hems, the strip would need to be 10 inches. If paper is used, it should be turned back like a hem and pasted down with a string inside to give strength to the edge. The cloth or paper should be glued fast to the outside edge of the long sticks. We start with two sticks first as shown in Fig. L, when dry the two sticks can be brought together, and the other two glued as shown in Fig. M. This gives an even spacing that otherwise would be hard to get. Such a kite can be rolled into small space and is very serviceable. It is easy to see that directions cannot be given for all the box kite class, but many articles have been writen on this phase of the subject, and by reference to the bibliography, no great difficulty should be encountered.

FIG. L.   FIG. M.

The triangular box kite can be compounded to quite an extent, but the tetrahedral has been developed by Dr. Bell until it can be made of any size, which is not true of other box kites. Some of the aeroplanes have a number of square cells in a series, with a number of adjustable planes for guiding purposes.

The making of box kites requires more real construction, and their lifting power is greater.

DRAGON KITES.

I cannot leave the kites proper without mentioning the dragon kites. They are a series of plain surface kites. The Chinaman devised a set of harness to make a lot of single kites pull together. They are not compounded, and not in tandem, but belong in a class by themselves. The connecting string, traces, or whatever they may be called, at the top and side and sometimes at the bottom should all be the same length between kites, so that when the head is tipped to the proper angle, all the sections of the body will be inclined the same amount. The Chinese dragon kite has discs for the body kites, but a very successful plan was adopted last year by using tailless kites throughout. The head can be some larger with the lower part of the covering (best of cloth) left loose and longer than the kite, like an apron, which blows back in the breeze like a beard. For this reason it is cut in irregular shapes. Very light splinters of bamboo with tassels of tissue paper on the ends, extending a few inches to the outside of the kites, can be used as balancers. These should be very carefully spaced. A dragon kite with a 3 ft. head and 2 ft. body kites, will prove very satisfactory. All the way from 6 to 15 body kites may be used with about 2½ ft. spacing between kites. The tail piece may consist of a rod about the width of the body kite, with streamers floating out behind. It will require a sturdy boy or two to operate such a monster. See the "American Boy's Handy Book" for the Chinese dragon kite.

The centipede kite is about the same in construction.

The drawings of reels should require no special direction. A broomstick makes a very good rod, but it is not large enough in diameter for the drum, so this must be built up.

The signaling and experiments in photography have been well set forth in articles given in the bibliography. Two photographs here presented, Figs. N and O, show what was accomplished by a lad twelve years old with a kodak on a kite string.

FIG. N.   FIG. O.

The "Yacht Race in the Clouds," by Nugent in *St. Nicholas* for October, 1900, should inspire any boy to work hard to win success, but it is no easy matter to make a successful yacht. We used a little different mechanism last year for our yachts, but there is still room for improvement. This year we used a beam for the yacht and a wire nail bent into the shape of a hook for the release of the sail. Some of the boys have attached light elastic, so that when the sail is released it will be pulled down quickly, thus expediting the return.

The tournament of 1907 was recorded in the MANUAL TRAINING MAGAZINE of December, 1907. The tournament of 1908 was a much greater success. Fully five thousand people were present, and the exhibition was worth going to see. All the participants were not registered, but 39 schools were represented, and 216 registrations were made. The air seemed full of kites—big and little, strong and curious. It was a sight to be remembered.

Much might be said about the streamers, messengers, wireless operation, etc., but we will close with just a word on the purpose and plan of the work.

The kite undertaking is encouraged through the schools, but is a home occupation. The construction is not carried on in the manual training shop, but is used as a supplement to shopwork.

The boy uses his knowledge developed in a manual training course in working out his own problems by himself. Mimeograph sheets were posted in each school with drawings similar to those presented here, for use as suggestions. The boys got their ideas, and worked them out during what would otherwise be idle hours. Many mothers have expressed their approval of the undertaking, and many teachers have been able to reach boys through this sport, that they were not able to understand before. The kite problem is seasonal. The tournament is brought about for the purpose of recognizing the efforts and success of the home occupation. There are many similar projects having as great variety as this one, that might be used in a similar way.

BIBLIOGRAPHY OF KITES IN PERIODICAL LITERATURE.

1. Competition of Kite Flying—Sci. Amer., June 13, 1903.
2. Craze About Kites—Cur. Lit., June, 1901; Tindal.
3. Construction of Kites—Sci. Amer. Supp., June 27, 1903; Bell.
4. Circus on a Kite String—St. Nic., July, 1902; Nugent.
5. Experiments with Kites—Cent., 32:78; Wise.
6. Exploration of the Atmosphere at Sea—Sci   .., Jan. 19, 1907; Roth.
7. Excursion with Kites—Cur. Lit., May, 1902.
8. Experiments by A. G. Bell—Sci Amer., May 2, 1903.
9. Franklin Kite Experiments with Modern Apparatus—Pop. Sci. Mo., 31:739.
10. Frost King (Tetrahedral)—Sci. Amer. Supp., June 1, 1907; Bell.
11. Festival of the Lantern Kites—Overland, March, 1907; Lorrimer.

12. Folding Malay Kites—Sci. Amer. Supp., Oct. 21, 1905.

13. Flexible Bridles on Kites—Sci. Amer., Oct. 6, 1900.

14. Hargrave Box Kite and Tetrahedral Compared—Sci. Amer. Supp., June 3, 1908.

15. How to Make Kites and Flying Gigs—Wom. Home Com., April, 1904; Adams.

16. International Kite Ascensions—Sci. Amer., Aug. 10, 1907; Ferguson.

17. International Kite Flying Contest—July 25, 1903.

18. Kites; Their Theory and Practice—Jo. Soc. Arts, 46:359; Baden-Powell.

19. Kite in Meteorological Research—J. Franklin Inst., 148:241; Marvin.

20. Kite in War and Peace—Chaut., 29:582; Welsh.

21. Kite Flying in 1897—Pop. Sci., 53:48; Varney.

22. Kites and Meteorological Observations—Nat. 55:150; Clayton.

23. Kite Flying, Scientific—McClure, 6:379; Moffett.

24. Kite as a Life Saver at Sea—Engineer Mag., 7:213.

25. Kite Balloon, Captive—Nat. 36:278.

26. Kite Flying as a Fine Art—World Today, Oct., 1907; Zah.

27. Kite Flying in Life Saving Operations—Sci. Amer., Mar. 9, 1907.

28. Kites in the Service of Meteorology—Nature, May 10, 1906.

29. Kite Flying in the East—Cur. Lit., April, 1901.

30. Kite Principles in Aerial Navigation—Sci. Amer., June 27, 1903; Serviss.

31. Modern Kite and Government Experiments—Outing, 30:43; Hunter.

32. Meteorological Phenomena on Mountain Summits—Sci. Amer., July 3, 1907.

33. Meteorograph Construction and Operation—Sci. Amer. Supp., Feb. 10, 1900; Marvin.

34. New Observation Kites Invented by S. F. Cody— Sci. Amer. Supp., Apr. 11, 1903, and Sci. Amer., Feb. 20, 1904.

35. Observation War Kites—Sci. Amer., June 13, 1903.

36. Photography from Kites—Century, 32:86; Eddy.

37. Picturesque Chinese Kites—Sci. Amer., Dec. 5, 1903; Beasley.

38. Scientific Kite—Spec., 78:576; Woglom.

39. Scientific Kite Flying—Century, 32:66; Millett.

40. Scientific Kite Flying—Independent, Sept. 27, 1900; Eddy.

41. Scientific Kite Flying—St. Nich., Oct., 1907; Claudy.

42. Signaling with Kites—Sci. Amer., Oct. 13, 1900.

43. Tailless Kites; How Made—Outlook, 58:1026; Briggs.

41. Scientific Kite Flying—St. Nich., Oct., 1907; Claudy.

45. Tetrahedral Kite in Wireless Telegraphy—Sci. Amer., April 21, 1906

46. Tetrahedral Kite—Cur. Lit., July, 1904.

47. Tetrahedral Kites of A. G. Bell—Pop. Sci., Dec., 1903; Grosvenor.

48. Tetrahedral Principle in Kite Construction—Sci. Amer. Supp., June 13, 1903; also Nat. Geog. Mag., June, 1903.

49. Traction by Kites—Sci. Amer. Supp., Sept. 29, 1900.

50. Use in Meteorological Observations at Sea—Sci. Amer., Dec. 31, 1904; Rotch.

51. Use in Meteorological Observations—Sci. Amer. Supp., Dec. 21-28, 1901, April 18, 1903; Oct. 13, 1900; Rotch.

52. Work with Kites by U. S. Weather Bureau—Nat. 63:108; Nat. Geog. Mag., 11:55.

53. War Kites—McClure, 12:543; B. Baden-Powell.

54. Yacht Race in the Clouds—St. Nic., Oct., 1900; Nugent.

WINDMILL KITE—TOURNAMENT OF 1909.

THE KITE TOURNAMENT.

In organizing a kite tournament some one person should take the responsibility of the undertaking as a whole. The supervisor of manual training would naturally be the best one to act as director. In case there is no manual training supervisor, the superintendent can appoint some one especially interested in boys' sports. It is not necessary to have a manual training system to start kite construction. The boys get their own material and do the work at home. In special case the sticks may be ripped out in the manual training room.

Some six weeks or so before the tournament, the director should send out the announcement. At least one copy of the instructions should be sent to each school. In Los Angeles four or more copies were sent to each school, and they had hard wear. If the occupation is encouraged in selected schools, a copy of the instructions could be placed in each room.

The principal of the school is the proper person to encourage the work of that school, seconded by the manual training teacher, if there is one in the building. It is good policy to use the principals and manual training teachers as judges as they will do more than other teachers to get out a good representation.

The first tournament should not be loaded down with too many feats. Perhaps eight or ten would be enough for a beginning. Los Angeles started with eight the first year, sixteen in three groups the second year, and thirty in four groups the third year.

Each school might have a "try-out" week before the tournament, but it should not be too near the tournament as the boys do not want to exhibit their kites then for fear they may be torn or that someone else may get their ideas and copy them. When the boys get to work in real earnest for contest, they work in barns, down cellar—some place out of sight. No kites for the tournament may be looked for in the air the last week.

SUGGESTIVE PROGRAM FOR THE FIRST TOURNAMENT.

Group I.—a. Most artistic kite; b. best decorated kite; c. highest flyer; d. strongest puller (to be tested by spring scales); e. best boy kite.

Group II.—a. Bird, animal, or insect kite; b. best invention; c. quarter mile dash (in which a boy lets out 1320 feet of string and winds it in again. Reels may be used to wind in. String must be measured before the tournament); d. reels; e. suspended banners.

Choose a place for the tournament that is free from wires, that has plenty of room, that is open to the breeze and is accessible to car service. See the street car officials that the car crews may give the kindest consideration to the kite boys. The street car company gets good returns out of it, so should be very considerate. A few policemen have a quieting effect on boys with inclinations to do mischief, and are also very serviceable in keeping back the crowds from some of the contestants.

Bulletin boards designating where the various feats are to take place, are of much service. These boards should be placed high enough to be well above the heads of the spectators.

The registration should be taken at the various schools by the principals the day preceding the tournament and should be turned in to the director the same evening. It is quite difficult to get a complete registration on the tournament grounds.

It seems best to so plan the tournament that all the kites may remain up during the afternoon, as it will probably be impossible to get the kites of one entry pulled down to give way to another. Then, too, there is a much better showing if all the kites can remain up all the time.

The boys should be encouraged to select the plain kites at the beginning, the tendency being just the opposite. The simple ones are much better for the study of the main principles of kite construction and flying. Until some ability has been acquired, the kite flyer cannot properly diagnose a case of kite delirium; he does not recognize simple defects, and may give up a good kite that is nearly a success. If some grown up boys who are acting as principals or instructors, would make an up-to-date kite for their own pleasure and the encouragement of the boys, it would strengthen a bond of fellowship wonderfully.

The foregoing sketch and notes on kite-making give enough to start the work of construction, but leave something for the boys to work out for themselves. The article is intended for suggesion, but stops short of complete details.

The greatest good is derived from the planning of the kites and the construction of the same, but the social gathering of the schools and the learning to abide by the judges' decision are valuable assets to the year's work.

Simple little diplomas, signed by the superintendent, chairman of athletic sports committee, and the director, recognizing superior exhibition of skill at the tournament, are much appreciated by the victors. It is possible that a silver cup might be used to good advantage as a trust to the school winning the greatest number of points, to be kept until the next tournament.

LOS ANGELES KITE TOURNAMENT.

The Third Annual Kite Tournament of the Los Angeles City School District was held April 3, 1909. It was a glorious day but the wind was quite uncertain, changing from a northerly direction in the morning to a southerly direction in the afternoon. The tournament began at about 2 o'clock; some of the boys brought their lunch and were on the grounds by eight in the morning. There was not sufficient breeze at the beginning to support the large kites and it looked quite discouraging, these kites only pulling about 2 lbs., but by three o'clock some of the kites began to break away and our fears were removed.

It was a magnificent sight when all the various creations of color, shape and energy were exhibited. The interest is ever increasing with both the children and the parents and a great assembly was present to witness the contest. Larger kites and more complex construction were attempted than heretofore. A good start was made on trussed construction and interest did not cease with the tournament. Many are planning to secure a prize next year. One kite had a windmill inside its frame which gave motor power to work a lever which caused a head to wag above the kite. One example of the sort is enough to start a whole new field of possibilities. Electricity will probably be used for a similar purpose next year. Simple diplomas stating the feat in which the contestant excelled were given to the victors. The diplomas were 5½ in. x 8½ in., printed with brown ink on a light tan paper.

SECOND PRIZE, ARTISTIC KITE—TOURNAMENT OF 1909, LOS ANGELES, CALIFORNIA.

A number of girls entered this year but do not like to compete with the boys except in artistic make-up and decorative features, so a number of feats exclusively for girls will be added next time. The small boy too is hard pressed and so a place will be given for fifth grade and under.

The spirit of the whole occasion was excellent—no bitter strife of one school with another—each child enthusiastic about the whole affair, and all the thousands of children, while excited, were genteel and happy.

Many a boy works on his kite for a month or more. At first, some of the members of the family will be very indifferent, but by the time the kite is finished, father, as well as the rest, is making suggestions, and they turn out in full force to see Bobbie win the prize. Sometimes the simpler kites with inexpensive materials are superior to the opposite. In nearly every case there is a very willing submission to the decision of the judges. In a race, one wins and the others must lose, so the children are learning valuable lessons for life in their own contests.

The larger boys try for the difficult feats of skill and strong pulling. Two kites seemed almost alike, but when the scales were applied one pulled 34 pounds while the other registered but 28 pounds. This comparison brought out further study in which it was found that one had a curve that the lighter puller did not have.

Only two yachts were in condition at the time for the race, then one of the kites kept breaking away so the one left made its ascent of 400 feet where the sail was tripped and the yacht spun down to its proud owner, making the round trip in about 2½ minutes.

Perhaps the most exciting feat was the quarter mile dash. Out of ten entries but seven started; the string was all measured and handed to the boys at the time for starting. Each boy was to start his kite, play out 1320 feet of string, and when it was all out he could attach it to a reel and wind it in as fast as possible. Each boy was entitled to one helper and they were timed by one of the judges. Policemen kept the crowd back from the lines. Very soon three kites were far in the lead, some getting mixed up, one failing to carry all the string, etc. See! one is at the end of his string and is winding in; now another is winding in; the third, soon after starting to wind in, catches his kite way out in yonder tree, and snap goes the string! The other two are working to their limit, one winding in a little over a yard at each turn; up the kites mount in the sky; now to this side, now to that; they are being pulled unmercifully. Now one is nearly overhead! Noisy? No; the excitement is too great to even yell. Here comes the first one right down with a bang on the heads of the spectators. It is not allowed to remain there, however, but is dragged right into the reel. The second follows hard after, and so the race is over. There was a prolonged yell about this time, Nat Stockwell of the Union Avenue School had won first place, and Elgin McNarry of McKinley Avenue second. The crowd about the boys shut off all breeze and to say that the boys perspired freely is putting it very mildly.

A real glider was brought on by one of the boys; it was very interesting at the time, and also instructive for next year's construction. An attempt was made to glide for a short distance but a gust of wind caught the aeroplane and forced one corner to the ground, snapping off a post.

One event looked very serious for a time but had no serious consequences. A lad had entered the wireless competition and had laid good plans; he had aluminum wire for a conductor from his kite and had the ground wire attached to a water hydrant. A gust of wind, however, snapped his kite loose and let the wire drop across the trolley wire.

AN OLD BICYCLE BROUGHT INTO SERVICE
IN THE LOS ANGELES TOURNAMENT.

When the kite broke loose he became confused and got tangled in his wire. The current was sufficient to stun him and he fell. As soon as he was removed he revived and was taken home immediately. The boy claims he did not have any bad effects from the schock. This is reported that others may be cautious how they handle wire kite lines near trolley systems. The program of the tournament was as follows:

Group I.—a. Bird kite; b. Insect kite; c. Artistic kite; d. Best decorated kite; e. Animal kite; f. Man kite; g. Suspended figures; h. Star kite.

Group II.—a. Strong puller (over 3½ feet); b. Strong puller (under 3½ feet); c. Yacht race; d. Quarter mile dash; e. Parachutes; f. Kite antics; g. High flyer.

Group III.—a. Balloon ascension (endurance); b. Balloon ascension (beauty); c. Wireless operations; d. Photograph from kite; e. Dragon kites; f. Aeroplane as kite; g. Real glider.

Group IV.—a. Smallest plain kite; b. Smallest box kite; c. Quick construction of kite; d. Kites with moving parts; e. Best invention; f. Reels; g. Windmill kites.

A few of the winners are shown by the photographs, but the colors are missing, a very important feature in the kite's appearance.

Books on the Manual Arts

Beginning Woodwork. At Home and in School. By CLINTON SHELDON VAN DEUSEN; illustrated by Edwin Victor Lawrence.

A full and clear description in detail of the fundamental processes of elementary benchwork in wood. This description is given through directions for making a few simple, useful articles suitable either for school or home problems. Even without a teacher a bright boy, by following this book faithfully, may acquire considerable skill. It is a safe guide for farmers' boys as well as for city boys, and is especially well suited for use in rural and village schools in which the teacher has had but little experience in the use of woodworking tools. The book is illustrated by more than one hundred figures, including ten plates of working drawings. Each of these figures is an original drawing made expressly for this book. Price, $1.00.

Essentials of Woodworking. By IRA S. GRIFFITH; illustrated with numerous pen drawings by Edwin V. Lawrence.

This is a comprehensive textbook on woodworking tools, materials and processes, to supplement, but not to take the place of, the instruction given by the teacher. The book contains three parts: I—Tools and elementary processes, including laying-out tools and their use, saws, planes and their use, boring tools, chisels, grinding and whetting, form work, laying out duplicate parts, scraping, sandpapering, and fastening parts. II—Simple joinery, including directions for making the common joints, elementary cabinet work involving drawer construction, paneling, rabbeting, and door construction. III—Wood and wood-finishing, including a great amount of information that should be given to a student along with his work in wood. The book does not contain a course of models. It may be used with any course. Price, $1.00.

Problems in Woodworking. By M. W. MURRAY.

A convenient collection of good problems ready to place in the hands of the pupils. It consists of forty plates bound in heavy paper covers with brass fasteners. Each plate is a working drawing, or problem in bench work that has been successfully worked out by boys in one of the grades from seven to nine inclusive. Many of the problems can be worked out in various ways according to the individual ability, interest and taste of the pupil. Price, 75 cents. Board covers, 20 cents extra.

Problems in Furniture Making. By FRED D. CRAWSHAW.

This book consists of 32 plates of working drawings suitable for use in grammar and high schools and 24 pages of text, including chapters on design, construction and finishes, and notes on the problems. Price, in heavy paper covers, $1.00. Board covers, 20 cents extra.

Problems in Mechanical Drawing. By CHARLES A. BENNETT. With drawings made by Fred D. Crawshaw.

This book consists of 80 plates and a few explanatory notes, and is bound in heavy paper covers with brass fasteners. Its purpose is to furnish teachers of classes beginning mechanical drawing with a large number of simple, practical problems. These have been selected with reference to the formation of good habits in technique, the interest of the pupils, and the subjects usually included in a grammar and first-year high school course. The book covers simple projection—straight lines and circles, problems involving tangents, planes of projection, revolution of solids, developments, intersections, isometric projection, lettering and working drawings. Each problem given is unsolved and therefore in proper form to hand to the pupil for solution. Price, $1.00. Board covers, 20 cents extra.

Books on the Manual Arts

Woodwork for Schools on Scientific Lines. By JAMES THOMAS BAILY and S. POLLITT.

This is the e   ing   problems designed to cor-
relate r them •   u   ing.   , 75 cents.

Clay W . .   y AATHERINE MORRIS LESTER.

This book covers the whole range of clay work for the elementary school—technique of clay modeling, study of plant forms, human figure, story illustration, simple architectural ornament, the making of tiles and ornamental pottery. Price, $1.00.

Classroom Practice in Design. By JAMES PARTON HANEY.

A concise, up-to-date, richly illustrated booklet on the teaching of applied design. Very suggestive. Price, 50 cents.

The Wash Method of Handling Water Colour. By FRANK FORREST FREDERICK.

"This little book is a helpful guide and affords a stimulus to the use of water-color as practiced by the earlier painters, whose beautiful work is unexcelled." Price, 50 cents.

Manual Training Magazine.

An illustrated, bi-monthly publication devoted to the interests of the Manual Arts in Education. Subscription price, $1.50 a year; single copies, 35 cents. In foreign countries, including Canada, $1.75 a year; single copies, 40 cents.

The Manual Arts Press
Peoria, Illinois

Made in the USA
Monee, IL
04 February 2022